Just Poetry

OrangeBooks Publication

Smriti Nagar, Bhilai, Chhattisgarh - 490020

Website: **www.orangebooks.in**

First Edition, 2022

ISBN: 978-93-5621-049-3

For the love of words

Just Poetry

Dr. Upma A. Sharma

OrangeBooks Publication

www.orangebooks.in

This book is dedicated to

My mother Ms Sumitra Gupta for being a constant source of inspiration, my Dad Prof. Anand Kumar Gupta for enlightening my path as I walked through different phases of life, my brother Vasu Aggarwal for his everlasting humour, my sister Jyoti Aggarwal for her unconditional love, my husband Ajit Sharma for soulful affection and my son Kartikeya Sharma, my heartbeat. I am also grateful to my friends for uplifting my spirits and not letting me put my pen down.

About The Author

Dr. Upma Aggarwal Sharma is doctor by profession and leads the Community healthcare programme of India's leading Pharmaceutical company under CSR. She did her MBBS from Govt Medical College Patiala and Post graduation in Health and family welfare management from National Institute of Health and family welfare, New Delhi.

She has a passion for poetry and has been writing since age of 13. She believes that penning is the only way to satiate appetite for words, words that remain tugged at heartstrings, unless subtly pulled, will not rhyme with the heartbeats. Positive words certainly are a way to serenity.

About The Book

This poetry book is a compilation of 101 poems, based on imagery, about bountiful nature, mighty ways of God that are toughest to comprehend, lifeline the family, soulful friends, amazing festivals, subtle sentiments, societal issues, moral and funny poems for children.

This poetry came out just from the love for words. Hopefully readers will be able to accompany the poet along the path created with her imagery.

The Preface

I reside in Chandigarh, India. Born in Talwara and brought up in Jalandhar, Punjab, I am the eldest child of my parents. Although three of us were in the same boat but expressed and reacted differently. I always used to write what I felt. When I was in 9th standard, one of my friends just peeped into my diary. I was 13 when I discovered that whatever I was writing, had turned to poetry.

I was writing just for the love of words.

To begin with, I wrote in Hindi and then started writing in English. These were on different topics and things of everyday life, some poems titled Mirchi (chilly) and Kaddu (pumpkin). During college days, my writing got refined and I wrote poems on Kalam (pen) and patriotism.

Almost a decade later, in 2013, I came across a wonderful group of poets at website poetrysoup and became a member. I started posting my poems and renowned poets from across the world started encouraging me by posting their views. I started learning about various forms of poetry and entered into various contests. My poems started winning top slots, and now that I have almost 1000 poems on the site, half of them have won in some or other contests. I started writing about the moon, the sun, the wind, flowers, snow, the sky, the ocean, the twilight, the seasons, the months, the God, the family, the friends, the festivals, relationship, the societal issues, moral and funny poems for children.

Some of my poems were also published in American online journals 'Whispers' and 'The Literary Librarian'. Two of my poems were also selected in Healing words competition & displayed during exhibition organised by company and charity "The advocacy project" in London.

Also I wrote on "Life during COVID times" which was published at company's website & also in our society's annual report, hence thought of publishing myself came to my mind and here I am.

I have tried to touch all subjects and many forms of poetry to express myself in this first anthology of my 101 poems.

I have felt and written as a daughter, sister, lover, wife, mother, friend, patriot, teacher, a child of God and as a citizen.

I am grateful to family, friends and God almighty for showering their blessings on me. I am quite hopeful and expect my readers to walk alongside my path during the rest of my journey with words.

Index

1

Sweet Morning

Golden beams of new rising aubade,
Fade away earlier day's weary jade;

An aura that fills the room with first ray,
Gear up yourself for bright brand new day;

First chirp of sparrows and clear blue sky,
Darkness flees, ending the night's spy;

Sunflowers bow their head to sunrise,
Roses and white lilies in garden add to surprise;

Fresh ideas in mind and a hearty zing,
Welcome another hopeful sweet morning !

2

Once The Covered Bridge

*Till last fine month
I was poising firm,
Aloft those giggling waters
that often went wild.*

*Taking pride of
my sinewy timbers,
As brimming loads of
endless desires passed by.*

*In my days of youth
condoned the avid,
Drudgery and ambitious,
Smirked evermore.*

*For years having allured
many adorable twosomes,
Charming familiar faces
grew up in grace.*

Now shattered I lie
beneath that aqua,
As feral waves caress
my deep wounds,
My tears sinking
tranquil to river bed.

Lost to negligence
my soul kept calling,
As soaked in edacity
you chose to be careless.

Once reckoning picturesque
was my enticing chemistry,
Amidst blooming greens
my stunning brown woodland.

Too late the realm
Severed beyond mend,
Now me, the covered bridge
be commemorated in history
and missed in panorama.

3

Crispy Leaves Of Autumn

as autumn sheathes in
red and gold of senescence ~
leaves do the talking

4

Listen To The Warm

As the chills of extreme winter bite me through the night, I close eyes to visit my memorable past when you held me in your arms so tight, I could feel your breaths on my neck, skin next to mine and thumps of fastened heartbeats.

Wantings craved to end tranquil as I listened to the warm.

I then open eyes to find no one by my side, frozen frigid with dried up eyes that do not reply to any emotion anymore, I wait endlessly for your eternal touch that only could send some warmth.

> Me and you and our rhythmic beats
> of that time were the soul's treat...
> Those close walls if were able to speak
> will evince and further endeavour to seek...
> How inseparable souls and crossed our hearts,
> could time ever tear us apart ?

5

There Is No Time
Like The Present

The only time you can embrace,
Moments lived in absolute grace;
There is no time like the present,
Not be wasted in discontent and lament.

With alpine mountains saluting you,
Vibrant seasons and countless vivid hues;
Nature as if celebrates every minute,
Why not honour the vast beyond compute ?

Digging the past and stay aghast,
Setting soul to uncalled for lambaste;
Or anticipating that future be bright,
And waking up in distress past midnight.

Inhale positive vibes of torrential flow,
Appreciate seven colours of the rainbow;
Now be the secret, now be the song,
As needles of clock keep ticking along,

Feel the mystic fragrance as of today,
Every today and each day after day;
If we could introspect and reinvent,
Be sure there is no time like the present.

6

Be At Peace

Conflict of societies,
Fight for boundaries;
Extreme collective aggression,
And we are at war .....

Ecosystem deteriorates,
Infrastructure crushed;
Modernisation of warfare,
Are we heading towards humanisation ?

Let one Tsunami rise
or an earthquake shudder;
And everything finally at peace.
To make us understand
that we, the inhabitants,
Only are visitors
And not born to own the land ....

Then why those mass graves,
Why the gunpowder;
And the nuclear weapons,
Learn some aesthetics and polemology ...

Let love wash internal rage,
And humanity tackle blood stains;
Altruism surface and nobility win,
So that birds can fly high
and animals enjoy freedom,
Ecology and greens flourish
as Mother Earth nurtures.

Serenity is in the air
to each soul's perfect flair,
Let logical reasoning grow
and Peace prevail ....

7

Dad

Only do I have fond memories
that often leave me teary eyed;
I wish clock could stop once,
to relive those moments, prized;

You were perhaps in a hurry
not to say us any goodbyes;
What more precious than kids
you must have anticipated dad;

No last words, no songs, we could
neither recall any wrongs;
Just an unsung desire haunts
when our very own taunt;

Many big and small laughs
soft heart and tender smiles;
A loving father's magic wand
sends blessings through miles;

Whatever we dreamt of
you ensured that turned true;
Many problems unsaid
often ended into faded hues;

Though your intense teachings
beacon our soul every bit;
Forever be our trailblaze
and keep our paths well lit.

8
Trees In Black

Down under the sky
Down under the tree
Tree stands tall
Tree ages old
Old leaves shed
Old thick trunk
Trunk wrapped in bark
Trunk tells the age
Age in years
Age it wears
Wears ancient look
Wears many nodes
Nodes are thick
Nodes deep brown
Brown vivid hues

Brown mixes green
Green grass surrounds
Green budding branches
Branches bear hive
Branches fast grow
Grow the flowers
Grow the fruits
Fruits get ripe
Fruits look fresh
Fresh fragrant breeze
Fresh cool mind
Mind that ponders
Mind sees beauty
Beauty of nature
Beauty of life
Life that begins
Life will end
End of desires
End of the day

Day that we lived
Day that descends
Descends down hills
Descends the sun
Sun that sets
Sun set twilight
Twilight lends orange
Twilight of dusk
Dusk spreads dust
Dusk progresses to dark
Dark engulfs colours
Dark means black
Black rules sky
Black of night
Night
Sky

9

Many Hues Of Green

Looking into her flashing green eyes,
Greener farming had only stayed with wise,
Queen's Emeralds if were seen,
Envy must have turned them green,
Unripe greens had to pay all the price.

10

When They Grow Up

My lonely house lays spic and span now,
no messed up clothes in cupboard bow;
All things lie still, where they belonged,
untouched, unmoved, staring at me as if ...

Knock at the door as I run to see,
no image moves with waves of wild sea;
Midnight whispers, wakes up the noisy breeze,
an empty chair watches those movies ...

Morning mirror counts wrinkles on my face,
years after years of counting days;
Smiles blossom as memories unwind,
to my cute little son's elegance redefined ...

To cherish those days I was occupied,
till sleep's embrace we could not sigh;
Those differences of opinion and fights,
trivial issues when got intensified ...

Who could imagine the time swiftly flied,
spin of fortune with every circle spied;
Bygone are exhaustion and agility of past,
tears of solitude engulf to tender soul's aghast ...

11

Where Frozen Embers Still Burn

Meeting you in life was an absolute delight,
Hearts rhymed perfect and eyes were bright;
Glow of a red blush on my face,
With your every blazing fiery embrace.

When souls took a far off flight,
There was a beauty even in the murky sight;
A tender heartache and you were there,
Those days certainly are lost somewhere.

Shunning the present and living in past,
Misery that would move the most obdurate heart;
No mold can shape as I quiver molten,
Memories of best times are frigid frozen.

Illusions of your breath every moment,
Diving deep into heart, flowing torrent;
Red running in my veins has turned auburn,
Frozen embers in my heart still slowly burn.

12
Coping Up With Life In COVID Times

Shake off all your fears,
have no doubts in His might;
You have come so far,
you can still go farther;

Like a river
that traverses through rough paths;
Like a mountain
that no hurricanes can move;
Like the Sun
that shines bright every morning.

Just like the darkness
of a frightful black night;
That comes and fades,
this too shall pass;

Stop for a while;
to take a look back in time .....

So many fond memories,
take some moments to cherish;
So many happy times,
revisit and rewind;
Feel the warmth,
of goodness of hearts;
Celebrate golden events,
Reverberate;
Recall beautiful upshots,
that intensely touched souls.

Enjoy the giggles of children,
and sarcasms of your spouse;
Stay close to parents,
once so rhymed your hearts;
Lyrics of a perfect home,
tuned to your dreams;
Pursue a hobby,
tickle your taste buds;
Take some rest.

For the precious breaths;
that await......

To seek tranquility in nature's lap,
lose to those subtle little chirps;
To meld into the luminance of Sun,
from aurora to twilight in the sky;
No longer on a high horse,
To be a part of the vast universe.

Stand the gaff
for being unjust to beings, to nature;

Be on the guard
and follow the rules;
Be with the warriors
redress the wrongs;
Show some mettle,
and you can fight fire with fire.

13

Song My Soul Sings

Why can't you hear,
it's afloat in air;
When it's gaining height,
look at the unique flair;

Some beats of my heart,
strong to say that, trust;
Few shy, sitting on cart,
Still will show you must;

My love for you is rising..
and I don't think it's surprising;

Why don't you feel,
the inside zeal;
When it's shouting loud,
Aren't you so proud?

Some strings that are plucked,
and smiles that are chucked,
Didn't all these set a rhyme;
A moment that is prime.

My love for you is rising..
and I don't think it's surprising;

Why don't you realise,
It's so clear in my eyes;
When it's not mere words,
Accept if you are no cowards;

Some breaths feeling so cold,
to skins although not old,
When alive is all the charm,
Why blood isn't that warm?

My love still is rising,
Don't you find that really surprising?

If it still be rising..
It's nothing surprising ...
Nothing surprising..

14

When Words Stay Silent

When thoughts get shrunken,
words remain silent,
When eye are sunken,
the tears gone dry;

When heart burns in betrayal,
love that dear denies,
When beats regress in depression,
passion pays a price;

The whole world comes collapsing,
no weapons, no fight,
Walking as a mere corpse,
the soul loses its might;

Nothing be done, Nowhere to go,
memories burden the mind,
Darkness, once aglow,
pretends to be kind;

Feel those skies calling
as morning sparrow chirp,
Wings of eternity,
May in time unwind.

15

A Martyr

No heading to a quiet peaceful one world,
Civilisations in name of development,
Producing the deadliest,
aiming towards end of human race....

You kill me, I kill you,
I defeat and conquer;
Souls tranquil rest in grace,
While no living ponder....

When patriotism asks for a price,
the price is a valuable human life ...

Father's elderly shoulders bear his weight,
A mother's affection melts into her eyes;

When brother's heart simmers on low flame,
And inconsolable sister silently cries;

His loving wife longing to meet,
sits on his coffin, draped in white;

Little arms that embraced around his neck,
hold fire to lit the father's pyre;

Warmth of brimming human emotions,
dumped in cold blooded patriotic ice...

A martyr
By own species...
Patriotism,
A dedication or
a frenzied outburst ?

Boundaries and freedom
Be mere words...
Man against man
Be not ultimate weapon...

A land that no one owns,
Is that for what we fight?
Defence or brutal sentiment of war,
Is there no looking beyond this sight?

16

The Others

*Amazing new house
and two little kids
that my husband left,
Losing life to war
yet wait him return.*

*Scared of some sounds
shadows of souls,
My daughter could see
through day and night.*

*They were five,
Haunted house?*

Shockingly,

*Not they,
Dead were*

We!

17

The Get – Together

Like crispy autumn leaves
tinged in vibrant orange hues,
that drop and freely float ;

Before settling for some rest,
Unless the breeze waltz
makes them dance to its tune.

We, the GOMCO 85, were,
rapt into lifeless routine,
Striving and working like Trojans;

Monotonous it might seem,
Yet content and tranquil;
mindful, sleeping like a log.

Until one great thought of reunion,
shook and woke us up;
A wave of delight traversed.

And there we all were;
together, meeting and greeting,
making some great memories.

Taken away by melody
of yesteryear songs ;
Had few refreshing Karaokes,
and countless rhythmic leg shakes.

The long sought soulful chats
having been vanished in time;
Those high pitched cheers,
lowered with softened profiles.

Broad day light dine,
and the sparkling wine;
Antakshari and adagios,
merging in essence of time.

Lost in aura of celebration,
a moment of parting came soon;
Embers of promises frozen in hearts,
waiting for fire to be lit again.

18

An Angel

Her angelic aura came as a prize,
affectionate heart kindled my soul
Succored a subtle mind mellow wise;

She would often set a noble goal,
for us to consummate and truly rise
Affectionate heart kindled my soul;

Aurora emerged into a bright sunrise,
muted deep, candid traits of humanity
For us to consummate and truly rise;

Forbearance supplemented the fragility,
In selfless sentiment, we were nurtured
Muted deep, candid traits of humanity;

Valiance in her core firmly structured,
Credence and perseverance twined
In selfless sentiment, we were nurtured;

God sent me mother as I whined,
Her angelic aura came as a prize;
Credence and perseverance twined,
Succored a subtle mind mellow wise.

19

Rakhi To My Brother

No distances can part,
no bearing can breach ...

As tender strings of rakhi,
I tie on my brother's wrist,
Send heartwarming wishes
to Illuminate those paths;
That we traversed together,
holding each other's hands.

He reciprocates with a gift
my fav he has always known,
Vows to stand by
in all thick and thin,
His pat on my back
and caress on head hearten,
Many nostalgic memoirs
recalled to brighten.

You my brother
I can always count on,

and lean on ...
Words fail me.

Those wonderful years
throughout my life,
spent in fun and pun,
Many blissful moments
some tears shed,
Laughter and scoldings,
Tiring little games,
Homework giggles,
lovely vacations together.

Cute hard chases
around in the courtyard,
Climbs of mulberry
amidst beehives,
Winning brought cheers
while losing gave sigh,
Etched in souls
are memories so sweet.

You my brother
Rise and shine,
Wish be the best ...
bubbling as always,
Sparkle forevermore.

20

Your Valentine's Day

Keeping off all eyes
as I plucked one red rose,
My heart thumped fast
he must be waiting for me,
Years after years
another thread of time,
Subtle memories ......

Valentine's Day
age no matter,
It was 2016
year no matter,
Driving faster
than heartbeats,
Till cheeks wore
that rosy blush ....

No diamonds could
glitter so bright,
No birds could
take such flight,
No stars could
bear that twinkle,
So serene was
no moonlit night ....

Losing myself
in his arms,
As youth smiled
exchange of beats
heard closer,
Tears of passion
rolling down,
I ceased to exist
as if one soul,
and I was all his.....

21

From Eyes Of A Kitten

As I wink my eyes through sun's bright shutter,
from beneath shrubs in lazy garden of the house;
I see vivid, iridescent blue butterflies flutter,
the youngest kitten, am not catching any mouse.

From beneath shrubs in lazy garden of the house,
numbered thirteen, only white among all black;
The youngest kitten, am not catching any mouse,
like swirl of petals, they chase me along the track.

Numbered thirteen, only white among all black,
floating gently in circles, land over my head;
Like swirl of petals, they chase me along the track,
I rub my paws, jump high to catch them instead.

Floating gently in circles, land over my head,
sweep untouched, sip on flowers and take flight;
I rub my paws, jump high to catch them instead,
hide in daisies to reappear on treetops in delight.

Sweep untouched, sip on flowers and take flight,
I see vivid, iridescent blue butterflies flutter;
Hide in daisies to reappear on treetops in delight,
as I wink my eyes through sun's bright shutter.

22

My Parting Gifts

I shall soon return
as your desires burn,
For emotions that bind
to soul's eternal grind,
So long there is scope
don't ever lose hope.

Alive in your memories
in your heart's core,
My intense love will flow
as rosy red cheeks glow,
Let grow the obsession
don't doubt my passion.

Trust you must ways to life
let go all unwanted strife,
His kindness, daily sunrise
sound sleep of dark night,
Even parting hearts throb
with twinkle of stars up above !

(Three parting gifts- hope, faith in my
love, trust in His kindness)

23

In A Perfect World

Mesmerising sunrise
to effulgence of moon,
Mysteries manifold
unveiling nature's boon,
Morning hymns
and melody of chirps,
Vibrant colours of flowers
as butterflies flutter,
Calm oceans depths
while rowdy seashores,
So much to cherish
to thrive and nurture,
Endless love and emotions,
His immense blessings,
We indeed are living
in a perfect world !!

But for the upcoming greed
cropping up selfishness,
The anger and animosity,
enmity going malignant,
aftermath wars.

Till we could awaken
incite kindness of hearts,
Rise above inequality
and shun digression,
Whip wild thoughts out
and embrace humanity.

To be truly living...
In a perfect world,
And in perfection !!

24

The Deadly Seven

Although engulfed in sea's stormy stride,
even the killer tides failed to eat false pride;

Living entirely in self, want and greed,
creating divide in name of colour, caste and creed;

Kindness, sincerity and love that were must,
through entire life we were wrapped up in lust;

No help came as ship dwindled for an anchor,
despair floated as we sank in our own anger;

As if born to live forever, nurtured gluttony,
  ate up resources and nature's harmony,

Sparked the green eyed monster in malignity,
  friends surpassing, blazing embers of envy,

Not working hard as the worthy, lying in sloth,
  losing effervescence and expecting froth,

Only if a man could shun the deadly seven,
  will open the golden gates to serene heaven.

25

Wool

Cozy and soft as
interwoven strands of wool,
Yet sending quivers,
passion storms coerce within,
Heart lends its warmth to the soul.

26

When I Will Be Gone

Memories will reflect in mirror of mind,
If at all in life you feel I were kind;
Nothing ever put in a secret box,
True feelings not meant to end in hoax,

Poetry books that must have gathered dust,
Shall unfold your favourite flower must;
Petals dried up in moments of sublime,
As fragrance of youth lies frozen in time,

Loneliness deepens with evening cries of cricket,
If in heavens I could send you a plane ticket;
Midnight blues and the wake up bell,
When cravings rise, should we burn in hell?

27
Christmas Magic

Clinquant faces when bear a joyous glow,
Huge trees, jingle bells, colourful candles,
Revive last year's zest to see Christmas snow,
Illuminated houses and dreams of angels,
Singing carols, we dance to perfect grace,
Till essence of love attains its peak flair,
Magical white covers on trees embrace,
As silky pearl snowflakes float in the air,
Spreading across walkways, it touches soft,

Magnificent shine with brilliant sunrise,
As beaming kids slide, tumble and fly aloft,
Gala fest spirit comes as no surprise,
Idolise celebrating till twelfth night,
Chasing innocent dreams that sparkle bright !

28

No Blank Pages

Some golden pages of life
forgotten in ruthless time,
Still waiting to be inscribed,
thoughts given an ink.

29

My Love Cars

My first rendezvous
was Honda Civic iVTEC
black automatic,
1799 cc, 4 cylinders
130 BHP, torque 172Nm,
Stole my heart
speed bound no limits,
Left me for a new owner.

Shunning loneliness,
Magnetised by
his macho shape
and pearl white colour,
Graceful eye to eye
luxurious costume,
I let his lusty belt
embrace my waist,

One button start
and we were together
Adrenaline gush
to a four by four,
Off road
over tough terrain
wondered his guts....
2800 cc, 4 cylinders
178 BHP, torque 350Nm,
Pajero Mitsubishi
my passion SUV.

Five years later
as it betrayed,
My heart cried
Grief of parting .....

Toyota Fortuner
my next fortune,
D- 4D, inter cooler
Turbocharger 2982 cc

168 BHP, Torque 343 Nm
Walked into my life
tough milky white,
Hugged me dear
wiped my tears,
My next love
its exquisite walk,

I try to escape those
Green eyed monsters
those road runners....

One Land Rover
Range Rover evoque
is now eying at me,

Waiting for
another heartbreak....

30

As I Suffer In Pink

My world came crashing down,
to know that I suffered cancer breast;
Having pink disease was such an agony,
Better had I been dead.

Why me ?
Had been so fit exercising,
Healthy food, taking lots of fruits and vegetables;
No tobacco, no alcohol, no drugs, perfect weight,
No family history in blood relations.

It was only while self examining my breasts,
A little lump my soft palms could feel;
There was nothing till last week,
In front of mirror while bathing I regularly checked,
or while laying with flat of palms I felt.

Then mammography and FNAC did prove,
Other tests to know the extent and spread;

My womanhood at stake
as I get them removed ?
I might not at all look sexy,
What would my man think
as I lose my magnetism ?
No no I better die !!

They say it's an early thing,
Quick early diagnosis
means a complete cure;
Surgery, radio, chemo....
May be my hair will fall...

They say I must put up a brave fight,
To this deadly disease
and prove it for others;
Not be the lone survivor
as many might follow me.

I am priceless for my family,
My man, my kids, my siblings and parents;
all love me, need me,
One life is all we know of
to cherish and to be loved;
It's through body emotion is expressed,
My pure soul is what completes me !

Made up my mind...
Ready for the surgery and treatment and follow up...
I am at war with cancer....

31

As Blessings Serenade

Only if mountains could lend me some height,
Only if morning sunshine could confer any bright;

Will then my heart beat for His forever glory,
or my colour would simply fade in pride;
and astound people that close-by reside ?
He wobbles turbulence in the wild sea,
chills out the fiercest of all blazing plea,
creating golden history in one stride.

beauty of nature
as fragrance poises in air,
Virginal chirp of sparrows,
Sinless pure colours
and tender pristine flowers,
Sing hymns in His reverence.

32

India

Impressive rich culture,
Intense architecture,
imbibe a sense of pride,
Ideation trumpets.
Intrepid patriots
indeed for motherland,
in vivid colours smile.

33

My Chandigarh

City beautiful as it is rightly named,
Greener pastures, treetops embrace;
Wider roads, traffic perfectly tamed,
Clean as could be, an absolute grace.

Rich in culture, hospitable and kind,
Draped in passion, the tender hearts;
We, the people, have got lucid minds,
Versatile sunrises give us daily starts.

Merry go rounds mesmerise our kids,
College cafes, pubs fascinate the young;
Beautiful garden where the elderly sits,
Our roots are deep, branches well clung;

History and heritage inspirit true goals
as twilight hymns imbrue into our souls.

34

Funny Haikus For Kids - 1

monkey snatches purse
you throw banana to him ~
he throws back your purse

saddle a wild horse
to jump on its back swiftly ~
else it rides on you

tree that offers shade
also might be nesting birds ~
blesses with droppings

playing in puddles
and muddy clothes by day end ~
how will you face mom

vegetarian
big zeroes in the notebook ~
is there any use

35
Arrives The Spring

Allure of raindrops
as drizzle knocks,
April arrives ...
Ecstatic Spring
ushers joy,
Buds bloom
petals unfold,
Vibrant colours
eyes behold,
Mustard in yellow
wheat gives gold,

Fragrant breeze
to lovers' delight,
Heavenly azure

and soaring flight,
Reigning blue
echoes into sea,

Festivals lure
delicacies to relish,
Step into May
with blushing
Red roses,
Luscious Mangoes
enticing delish,
Basking days
evenings coldish,
Verve satiates
soul's every wish!

36

Who Are You

*A fragrant breeze
to be felt close,
The sweetest red rose
cuddling its origin,
Kindest of heart
that has a healing touch,
Reflector to sunshine
and nurture positive mind,*

*All what I am not
and just trying to be..*

*But surely I am ...
A nature lover
pleading to preserve its beauty,
A human being*

far from hatred just caring,
A heart that believes
in equality for all life,

Longing for ...
peace and not wars,
no discrimination to colour
caste and religion,
no exploitation or killing,

Am I a theoriser
an idealist or an escapist ?
For readers to decide ...

37

Equations

Linear array of
life symbols,
If one could set forth
on left and to the right;
A mere balancing
of algebraic equation,
We swing to tunes
pulleys struggle a balance.

Unlike free birds
that fly limitless,
Confident cricket
that shrills constantly;
Bees humming
still their honey lost,
Flowers perishing
leave fragrance in air,
All celebrate life
no equations saught.

Man wasting
efforts and time,
Interfering into
laws of nature;
Killing and exploiting
in name of equations,
Nothing set right.

Let learnings
of physics, chemistry
and mathematics,
Apply to real living
Equations of love
and laughter,
Wisdom and speech
emotions and trust
Be congruent.

38

Breathtaking

Before I could see the glitter of rising sun,
Rays of his love had blinded my vision,
Enraged tides constantly swayed my thoughts,
As crescendo of rhyming beats rose high,
Trusted promises that drummed into temper,
Head could merely record songs of passion
Till plucked strings of violin were put to rest.
And there I was pondering, sitting aloof,
Kindness having walked all through the rough,
Is there a chance to relive if wrongs undone,
No matter how breathtaking the rope walks seem,
Gifts of fortune can't eclipse a shattered dream.

39
Those Were The Moments

Serene white clouds ...
that you are hiding behind,
Take me, take me with you..
Stars that twinkle
and shimmering lights,
Are sweet remembrance of you...

Dark was that night
your lips kissed mine,
and skies that went blue ....
Blazing moments
of passion that set us blaze,
Tears of parting I wonder melted only few.....

My heart that beats fast
your shadow I long to see..
Desires pretend a smile
Take me, take me with you..

I can't live here furthermore
If it's not with you ....
Ah the sweet remembrance
and beats rhyming in you ...

Take me, take me with you..
For how can I live,
For how do I live,
For why should I live,
Ah those eternal moments
That sweet remembrance of you ....

Those missed beats
as my soul craves...
Quench the thirst
and embrace those shapes.
Help me die, take my spirit,
Ah the sweet memories,
Those were the moments,
Those were the moments...

40

Who Are Those Funny Poets

Be it Jack Ellison or Jan Allison,
their witty pens invariably giggle,
Eileen's passionate words set ablaze
Dave's love lyrics urge us to dance.
While Paul's imagery leaves in awe,
Nette and Andrea trick with riddles,
Linda and Skat the souls of soup,
Carrie's creative brush paints vivid
Frederic lends throbs to emotions
Richard's positivity puts to dance,
Hats off to romantic Tim and Olive
Constance dips her nib in ink of heart.
Judy places at number one to shimmer
Silent one and Rob bestow fortunes,
Missed are Carolyn's wise words
and Dr Ram Mehta's brilliant fun writes.

41

Leonardo Da Vinci

Great painter of Italian Renaissance,
Unquenchable curiosity,
Human anatomy his fav,
engineer and scientist,
Sculptor and inventor,
Illegitimate,
Most eclectic,
polymath,
Unschooled
Whiz.

Dr. Upma A. Sharma

42

A Child's Home

Running in the courtyard
when sun is at its peak,
Harsh voice of grandpa
as he would sneak;

Long hours with friends
as play doesn't tire,
Books don't fascinate
and mother spits fire;

For watering of the garden
we are in a queue,
Hand pump crackles
with a rusty hue;

Dining room fragrance
as mother cooks my fav,
Jealous are others
favouritism is nothing new;

Oh the bedroom I share
with my bro and sis,
Cartoon time please spare
TV remote I crave;

Sound of train passing by
as window panes rattle,
In sleep I travel afar
to return to wake up alarm;

*Who likes to leave early
for lessons at school,
No time for splashes
that I cherish in the pool;*

*Recall the greater aplomb
in my childhood home,
No worries, no enmity
purity at heart, integrity;*

*Memories chase dreams
in morning screams,
When croaks the raven,
child's home is a heaven!*

43

It Were You

It's been ages as I wait,
moments frozen in my silvery plaits;
Years be counted in my wrinkles,
passion shines as hope twinkles.

Autumns returned in the orange hue,
as crispy leaves cherished their due;
Vibrant flowers in mesmerising cover,
Wished it were you back every summer!

I waited as perished every flower,
and sweet fruits all turned sour;
Yellow leaves swiftly bid adieu,
Turned at knocks to find it were you !

Many autumns passed by
to the sweet lovers convoy;
As I reeled in worst of fears,
my emotions shuddered in tears,

How long ! How long do I wait ?
with brush of youth, I colour my plait;
And camouflage smiles with wrinkles,
to find if life the soul can sprinkle.

As breeze renders me a soft caress,
tranquil in time our breaths coalesce;
Raindrops to tune of our hearts will rhyme,
Sure it must be you teaching mime!

44
In Love With Pirates

When titanic sank,
we were on the deck,
The boat did rescue us afar,
destiny had in store a new avatar;

The ship we asked help for,
lately been captured over,
Pirates killed kids and men,
sparing only few women;

Ugly faces, red eyes and shabbily dressed,
killer instincts, hatred be guessed,
Tears down the cheeks, my heart bled,
Days in captivation, breathing half fed;

Agony put to end with new pirate friend,
all different stories I could comprehend,
The day captain said his sad tale,
Catching up, I was no more frail;

Months passed as I lost my cool,
Tough ordeal, life dwindled in blood pool,
Countless shots even with my gun,
Pirate captain now is my only son!

45

Dora And Cheeku

Charming pair of brave dachshunds,
Very possessive and stubborn,
Grew up with my only son,
Envious of my love for him;

Running around was a part of play,
Rolled and giggled the whole day,
Ignored if, they would sit in a corner,
With drooping faces of a mourner;

Day, burglars broke into, was calm,
As thief ran to their wake up alarm,
Took cheeku away along with them,
Dora kept digging garden crying for him;

No foods or feasts could console,
Even the police failed to prove their role,
We died each day with her rising passion,
Loneliness had turned into obsession;

Till she too disappeared the other day,
After turning garden into a heap of clay,
Parting was unbearable to our hearts,
Tears of grief tearing our souls apart;

Comical clowns that once gave us smiles,
Must have found peace or travelled miles,
Memories haunt as those lovely days we recall,
Adorable pets, I still feel them leaning against the wall.

46

Power Of One

One of the kind,
One in a million,
Can we be the one ?

One eyed, one legged,
One rich, one poor,
Can we be of one mind ?

One hell of a fight,
One day you will be sorry,
Maybe......

The evil one,
The holy one,
First and the last,
One and only,
Devil, Satan or God ?

One regret,
One achievement,
One sided love,
Be one up on,
Does one opinion count ?

Unique
Cardinal
United
Solitary
Is the power of one
His infinite power !!

Each soul merges
in one macrocosm,
Single vast sky
beyond this earth,
Floats serene into
one universe !!

47

Putting On The Ritz

Those weird faces
below glamorous make up,
The enormous laughs
under those debts,
Show off to whom
lesser privileged than you?
As those affluents
will never look at you !

Luxury of the motels
and wine in pubs,
Those night lusts
and hefty gifts,
Moving in bigger cars
owning king sized houses,
Best of attire
embellished in sapphire,
False faces of ritz
truth dumped deep within.

Whence our kids
crave for foods,
And poor naked in streets
are covered only in mist,
Longing for a meal
as hunger eats mankind.

Why can't we be modest
to accept in dignity,
When at the lounge we stand,
Counting our guests
wishing there was a miss,
Showing liberty at heart
that weeps on money shed,
Hard earnings wasted
on an imitation game,
Pocketed inside out ersatz,
Putting on the Ritz!

48

See Through My Eyes

Cheerful faces
with my first cry,
Born into this world
my mother's pretty face,
Forgetting all the pains
thrived with all grace,
Saw through my little brain
everyone in a rat race,
Hurt, insult and abuse,
world was no holy place,
Kids and women killed
bloodshed their real face,
Lavish spending on wars

while hunger begged at sacred place,
Brutal murders and rapes
of humanity, law and jail breaks,
Mother Earth exhausted
of its natural resources,
Selfishness, greed and cruelty
I am so much scared,
Days are dark
and nights awake,
Take me to a safer place mother
maybe back into your womb,
Afloat in peace with my eyes closed!

Dr. Upma A. Sharma

49

Jealousy

I grinned as they laughed
as if making fun of me,
The lesser child of God-me,
Their inseparable love
Why could I not get?
Fortune smiling at them
and mocking at me,
Born with a silver spoon
Why not me?

A luxurious life style
lavish dinners,
Adored by all
gleaming shimmers,

Beauty with a kind heart
at peak of fame,
Why not me ?
Was I born with those
green eyes?

A fright to laughter,
An injured lover's hell,
Cruel as a grave,
Stronger than love,
Well is that jealousy?

My suspicious fears
and envious resentments,
Turned to a jealous rage
kept me burning inside,

Poetry doing top honours
wish were truly mine,
Hard work put by a friend
why hope win was mine ?

Oh envy!
Thy name I can't see,
I can't let that green eyed monster
ever feed on me !

Introspection
Rumination
Meditation
Will these cure my disease?
Will it change colour of my eyes?

50

Waiting

Years have passed by
as I endlessly wait,
Sure you are at peace
crazy... that's my trait;

Life a dejected flute
that you no longer hold,
Its many holes waiting
for your tender kiss;
Warm breath to be blown
inside of me,
Magical melodies ...

Those loving moments
longings that got buried,
Waiting to erupt
anytime passion volcano,
Molten smooth lava
to unleash my desires,
Asleep on flames ...

Drumming beats
of a broken heart,
Losing all rhythm
waiting to be mend,
My soul you took along
a mere body now crawls,
Abraded bleeding ...

Faint colourful images
treasured deep within,
Spirits that intrigue
for all times to come wait,
Be sung as regional songs
those tragic tales of love,
Glorious pages of history...

51

To My Mother

(From perspective of a son)

How could I forget
the pain she took for me,
Bringing me into this world
to savour life in glee,
Fed on her blood and milk
as I opened my eyes,
Her heavenly smile erased
my tears and intense cry;

Nurtured with selfless love
I was no more a boy,
She is still my dream girl
though her youth has passed by,
Gracious grey hair
maturity of thoughts,
We recall fun and giggles
on many funny plots,

She knows all my wants
and every moment I sigh,
Strong emotional bond
always been my pride,
Her one touch
and mountains can move,
Possible without wings
flight she can prove,

Salute to all women
as I grow into a man,
Mother, the procreator
His best creative plan,
X of her strength I inherit
in my each cell,
My role model she is
inspires me to excel!

52

Ill Fated

Life was so smooth
until one condemned evening
They bundled her up in a van
and then took to a deserted place;

She could sense her misfortune
to their sarcastic smiles,
A sense of hatred and agony
watered clear in her helpless eyes;

Treated as a vegetable
for no fault of hers,
Stripped of her modesty
was it a male pride ?

Five of them and her subtle being,
not a stitch on as the body shivered bare,
Hunger for flesh, scarring the soul,
wonder her strength to survive that scare;

Not a human being, she was just a consume,
rights can we talk as insane hooligans roam ?
Pity them for the crime not so heinous ?
or punish for murder of the soul as well ?

Unconscious they threw her on road to die,
to hospital she was taken by a passer by,
There was no end to the ill luck,
label of a rape victim dumbstruck;

Inquests, courts and then the ugly game,
in name of law, it was such a shame,
Her bubbly heard bled, stabbing cry,
Ripped soul could heave no sigh;

An year now, guilty roam free as tears burst,
as if females are born to quench their thirst,
Why not teach our sons to respect?
Ill fated or is it our bringing up neglect?

Quick justice the need of the hour,
she is no lust, she is a man's power,
Can sons ever prosper at daughters' price?
Hold the flame high against gender crime rise!!

53

I Went To Heaven

Cherishing an opulent living in world,
anticipating a front seat in heaven,
I was made to believe that Yamraj will send
a white chariot taking best of souls up above;

Where Dharamraj with scroll of our work
will give a final verdict on ranking,
And pronounce a heaven to the one
who pursued life with spiritual karma.

But to my surprise ....
I only died to introspect,
All goodness gave me joy
grief was all the unwanted,
Realm of no heaven or hell
as my soul wandered,
How in life we fought on caste, religion and creed,
As if it would take to reign in heavens
and satiate an ominous afterlife greed.

Nothing I was empty handed,
no riches, no comforts taken along,
Barely anything above serene clouds,
No fairies or gardens of paradise,
Just a soul afloat with lifetime turned to ashes;

Mind the only reaping land,
ideas sowed in cognitive bruit,
Cruelty and cheat the hell,
heaven the karma of kind hands,
Content the ultimate divine fruit.

Dreaming ending into the actual,
by the crude croaks of raven,
Wondered having construed factual,
I went actually through my inner heaven!!

54

Hopeful

Whispers in the corridor heard louder and closer,
as security man asks relatives to leave,
In recovery room post operative patients wait,
docs are on their way for morning round,
many queries unanswered pop up in minds.

breathes freshness in air
a tender bird spreads its wings
squirrels hop around

Mother is apprehensive to know about prognosis
as her only child suffers cancer for last two years,
bubbly charm lost in deep ocean of pain,
if playful school days could be back again ?
teachers return with bagful complaints
of the naughtiest one.

a bright new sunrise
buds in vibrant colours bloom
shines the morning dew

Hope like a colourful feather floats in air to tempt
as they humbly pick and hand over to the mother,
her eyes twinkle, tears reflect the dazzle,
grateful to God for those kind healing hands,
He sent from heavens nourishing many souls.

the perishing seeds
saviours water in time
green revolution

55

Red Roses In The Garden

Somber thoughts clouded my mind
as I sat calm on the garden bench;
While parting as a prickly thorn
pierced my tender gloomy heart;
Till the soul rested in tranquility
and stained all the roses dark red.

56

Funny Haikus For Kids-2

croaking sounds calling
as you jump into puddles ~
frogs leap on your feet

little sparrows chirp
fly together as you tease ~
droppings on your head

giant elephant
trumpets and shakes its big ears ~
roller coaster ride

giraffe eats high leaves
wish they soon reach the stomach ~
stuck in the long neck

cartoons the whole day
animals play in jungle ~
as you watch tv

57

Late For Marriage

Loneliness engraved deep into my heart, I now am a mere stone. Many springs bloomed and autumns saw greens turn into orange, twilight of dusk brought no light of love as years passed by. No better than a piece of brain, I am work and all work. Ended the wait for the Prince Charming with dumped unsung unrhymed notes and plucked strings of subtle heart.

Try not mend my violin
those threads of thoughts
and hollow heart,

Try not steam my mind
those foggy images
in time forgotten,

Try not set ablaze
those dousing embers
for years frozen,

*As I love my freedom
own ways with life,
As I have no feelings
to be someone's wife,*

*Asking buds to blossom
know the time lag,
Faded colours if shine
I might not go blind,*

*Words that were lost
under covers of time,
Don't unveil to set free
for everyone to see,*

*My embarrassment
of learning so late,
Marriage was never my fate,
I want to be just myself.*

भारतीय डाक
INDIA POST

58

Autumn Fire

Veils of orange and red
camouflage in season,
Quenched intense heat
in chills set to quiver,
yellow leaves turn crisp,
swing and dive,
Aroma of Liberty
taking them to roads,
Rugs on walkways,
splendid arras,
Embers set ablaze,
embrace the Autumn fire !

Dr. Upma A. Sharma

59

Golu And The Bird

With twinkle in his big eyes,
With sharp nose and chubby cheeks,
With ears big as an elephant,
With kindness in his pure heart;

Golu was going to school,
Golu sang a sweet song,
Golu was getting wet in rain,
Golu was hopping on the road;

He heard shriek of a bird,
He followed it close,
He took off his hat,
He put the little bird inside;

The bird puffed its feathers,
The bird rolled its eyes,
The bird opened its beak,
The bird lay on one side;

His friends were happy to see,
His friends brought water,
His friends got some grains,
His friends kept it cozy;

Mother was waiting for golu,
Mother hugged golu on return,
Mother saw the little bird,
Mother asked golu to return it to its mom;

He set him free at same place,
He saw its mother sitting in wait,
He saw them chirp in joy,
He happily went to school;

When he opened his book,
When he read the chapter,
He recalled his own story,
It read 'Golu and the bird'!

60

My Boy

When he first opened his subtle eyes,
first ray of sun as if lit my morning sky;

Withered away the pain of all my life,
with inception of his one pleasant smile;

Soft caress and fingers in thin silky hair,
aura of twilight was his endless flair;

Pearl drops were his tears in a row,
ended always in iridescent rainbow;

Inseparable even though a cut cord,
a rhyming melody that my soul adores!

61

Pierce My Heart

Taken me granted, all my love,
you don't bother much,
Was so sure, from very first day,
those moments we intensely shared...

All that was mine, is now yours,
denial now, will be unfair,
Lost everything, was not my destiny,
in memories I live today, how far....

Thoughts depress, I must confess,
was a fool, from that first day,
Tears once kissed my rosy cheeks,
rosy red, rosy once, have dried today,
Why did you do so.....

What better will you ever get,
get up now, see me now, to later regret,
For I am the one, I am the one,
everything for you, anything for you......

Lived for you, can die too,
have a needle sharp, edge aim at me,
Cut me through, pierce my heart,
Test my wild rush for you,
and bleed my passion through and through......
See your name splashed over floor,
Pierce my heart, further squeeze,

You now have a stony heart,
why have you become so hard....
Burn me, chop me, crush me, tear apart,
Oh your laughter makes my soul weep
You are not the one.....
You cannot be the one.....

62

My Sweet Childhood

Oh this classroom of August,
Oh the heat and humidity,
Oh the teacher still taking lessons,
Oh such thick book and a long lesson,
Oh nothing going into my head,
Oh let them teach.. bla bla bla;

Can anyone tell what use it will be?

I will get good scores mom says,
I will get good ranking in exams,
I will be selected for higher studies,
I will get a good job,
I will get good money,
I will live happy further after;

May I tell you what am I losing now?

My little childhood joys,
My plays with the toys,
My lovely playground,
My desire to sing and dance,

My desire to meet friends,
My desire to google on tab,
My desire to download;

Am I not losing my present?

Take me to the sea so vast,
Take me where breeze blows fast,
Take me to the greener earth,
Take me to garden of flowers,
Take me where love has no dearth,
Take me where birds freely fly,
Take me where animals play hide and seek;

Let nature be my classroom and God my teacher!!

Let Him teach me fly sky high,
Let Him teach me climb mountains so rough,
Let Him teach me dive deeper in sea,
Let Him drive me into right emotions,
Let Him give me lessons on humanity;

Is there any teacher greater than Him??
Hence don't show me books and school!!

63

As Years Pass By

Growing up fast year after year,
Shine the pearls of my eyes;
But for funny face in mirror,
Smile comes at a price.

Watching squirrels hopp and pass by,
While endless anxious wait;
Running after him to ask why,
Now stick syncs with my gait.

Swinging trees from my window seen,
Breeze that brings his essence;
As time flies, memories umpteen,
Trick me on his presence.

Drizzling drops to the soul that soothe,
And make hearts go crazy;
Sizzling weather in gala mood,
I keep sitting lazy.

Moonlit nights and morning dewdrops,
Ah those silent crushes;
While pulse occasionally drops,
Now I have hot flushes.

Growing up fast year after year,
Shine the pearls of my eyes;
But for funny face in mirror,
Smile comes at a price.

64

Queen Of Hills

Alluring elegance of Simla, the queen of hills,
Morning pleasant breeze, at night gives chills;

Snow clad mountains, silvery charming shine,
Tall Deodar trees, dense forest, also few Pines;

Aromatic flowers garnish nature's platter, vividly grow,
Rivers run smooth; at times exhibit a turbulent flow;

Soulful scenic marvel, must artistry come alive,
No artist or poet here can ever fail to thrive;

Green valley on one side, hilly serpentine road,
As summer sun peaks, it is my heavenly abode!

65

Memorable Vacations

Queensland was a dream come true,
Along forest lake walks under the blue;

Summers of December 2010 on my sis' invite,
Excited we were for the double delight;

Long travel concluded into a toast,
Beaches and sea, Byron bay and Gold Coast;

Gold of sand slipped under our feet,
Glittered in sun the irresistible greet;

Waves that thrashed on us with every tide,
Engulfed us after a roller coaster ride;

Kangaroos that into every street hopped,
To give them way every now and then we stopped;

People were humble and kind,
Serpentine roads turning blind;

Sunny day we visited famous sea world,
Dolphins with music in unison twirled;

Kids together on giant wheel screamed,
Watched favourite movies and gleamed;

Train travel and beauty of countryside,
River Brisbane traversed with ferry ride;

Sydney opera house, bridge and harbour,
New year eve with fireworks and great fervor;

Days of goodbye when approached near,
Subtle emotions flowed and rolled the tears;

As we close our eyes and reminisce,
Days spent together were such a bliss!

66

Computer Dear

Everyday when I switch on my computer,
I say to myself,
Gets up from sleep at my one touch,
Recharged, he appears with a huge smile,
Is he in love with me?

Taking all my commands throughout the day,
And still giving his best,
Eye to eye without a flicker,
Working with me in unison,
I have the keys to his heart,
As he unlocks my brain;

Takes me to google,
And we travel around the world,
Keeps me updated what come may,
One button click and its a child's play;

Anything that becomes obsolete,
He helps me by selection of delete,
Each data that will sincerely behave,
I am able to place it under save,
He is my work passion, a must obsession;

Modern life, technology will surely steer,
There's no life without you computer dear!

67

Tell Me – Telling God

Mysterious indeed are His ways,
He creates all life to run smooth and then sways,
We, the puppets keep dancing at His will,
Though pretend having gained an immense skill;

Shaping the whole world in full grace,
Of the Unseen, who can create His face?

Try finding Him in every life,
By our side He's in each joy and strife,
Else why do the busy day's end,
Nights to quieten in peace He sends;

In no religion and places is He found,
Lives inside every kind heart that beats around;

Faith is God, belief is God, love is God,
Cheating yet preaching are all fraud,
Apart from all colours, cast and creed,
He is the one to be consciously perceived!

68

New Year

When new year resolutions at the eve
shatter in shimmer of next day's sunrise,
Setting sun's aurora if could forgive
Promises unkept waiting to fulfil,
beauty of dawn takes up as a surprise,
Grudges of past lost to desires that chill.

End up in dreams to be unveiled in time,
Some golden moments we fondly cherished,
in few years of life that were utmost prime,
Achievements studded in crown of glory
still far was content to be embellished,
New year nurtures hope, another story.

When new year resolutions at the eve
end up in dreams to be unveiled in time.

69

Calls Of Humanity

Denial to live a full and free life,
Segregation on creed, colour black or white,
How much tolerance must have been,
A call for human dignity and end of strife;

As came the South African apartheid,
A blot on developing intellectual breed,
Women and children could not escape abuse,
Human rights were not getting any heed;

No jobs, no food, such was the plight,
Even most educated had a pitiable fight,
Imprisoned without trial in unsanitary conditions,
Most horrible was the inhumane sight;

Mandela took a lifetime struggle to rescue,
All false allegations were taken true,
Then first election of universal suffrage,
How the time turned, had a least clue;

Defiance campaign with nonviolent resistance,
Task undertaken with strong persistence,
Pursued racial equality and other human rights,
Dilemma of democracy was coexistence !!

YAMAHA
408930C

70

A Child's Sky

Subtle emotions in heart,
till he grows up real smart,
Tears scroll down the chubby cheek,
for a toy meagre and meek!

Steals eye to slip out of house,
dad's anger is tough to douse,
The joy of winning marbles,
soon withers with growing barbels!

Mom is after for the meals,
not eating, puts her on heels,
Annoyance that ends in love,
Countless blessings from above!

Courage and zeal see no dearth,
angel gets heaven on earth,
Holy soul knows no deceit,
a child's sky has winsome fleets !!

71

Twilight Hues

serene morning sky
wake up to the twilight hues ~
subtle sparrows chirp

72

Periodic Table Of Elements

Periodic table of elements,
the true heart of chemistry,
Law of periodicity clements,
Mendeleev is not a history!

Bonding between two hearts,
ignoring all the negatives,
When breaks and rips apart,
defying the electro positives;

Atoms randomly disperse,
Directionless, blinded and betrayed,
Valencies in their course traverse,
Swaying in the numbers brigade!

73

Golden Days

Reminisce those golden days left far behind,
Little joys lived to most, recalls the mind,
Aiming sky high and free as birds,
Cherished life, simple were our words;

Childhood friend at primary school,
Waited daily for me but I was such a fool,
One reserved seat for me always next to him,
Ignored the passion till it flowed to brim;

Teased others as together we grew,
Till medical school, left were only few,
Hostel life was more of a fun,
Witty siblings added to real time pun;

Affection of parents in family of five,
Pretty house, floral garden, fruits and beehive,
Bright sunrise to twilight of sunset,
No hues were missing in my palette;

Delicacies that my mom cooked,
Anyone who ate got really hooked,
Carom, cards and chess that my dad laid,
Losers tried till years and decades;

Reminisce those golden days left far behind,
Little joys now unseen, have I turned blind?

Dr. Upma A. Sharma

74

A Christmas Snow

Festive spirits at the faces glow,
Glitter in the eyes and joys flow,
Bells ring, carols sing, chill will stay,
A Christmas snow is on its way!

Pure white to tall trees embrace,
At roofs of houses sways in full grace,
Covering all walkways look so soft,
Children cheerful seen flying aloft!

Everything having been put in array,
Angelic touch that melts it away,
Divine chaste coming from heavens,
Reflecting life's perfect sevens;

Vibrant colours various hues,
And we forget our past blues,
Illuminating hearts are the lights,
Mesmerising charm of the bright;

Falling snowflakes floating in air,
Essence of love catches its flair,
White will sharpen with each sunrise,
A Christmas snow comes as a surprise!

75

Christmas Dreams

A whole year long wait,
and Christmas is here,
Cheerful faces and dancing gait,
Must enjoy its fragrance in the air!

Remember gifts of last year,
Santa to our dream as we exactly thought,
Promises that were done for this year,
Let's see what special he has now got!

Time to get ivy, holly and mistletoe,
Jingle bells, candies and colourful candles,
and wait for cover by a pure white snow,
Lighted houses, illuminated sleighs and angels!

Paint the chimney new for Saint to creep in,
and slip gifts into stockings hanging by fireplace,
At night when the church bell will ring,
Carols will add melody to festive's grace!

Will take celebrations to the twelfth night,
And wake up with dreams shining bright!

76

Cowboys In Badlands

When the horses refuse to move further,
And the sunset pours its gold all over,
Cowboys determined see only their goal,
Nothing can stop them listen to their soul;

Riding on back, they set the saddle,
Prepared to face bravely each hurdle,
Sun goes further down, auburn turns gold,
Nothing can scare them, hunger nor cold!

Drying breeze as far as eyes can see,
No sign of water even birds will flee,
Passing through the hills and lands barren,
Nowhere to be seen beasts or fowls of warren;

Badlands as if are hallmark of cowboys,
Nothing can deter them, no when and whys!

77

Snowfall

As the snowflakes slid down in air,
the winter resumes its perfect flair,
Our warm breaths smoke,
the frozen engines choke;

Shiver smiles in conditioned rooms,
stars wink to the hearts in gloom,
White cover gives a tight embrace
shining to bright sun's morning grace;

Snow capped mountains and trees enthral,
As passion heats up the mystic snowfall.

78

The Raven

Walking slowly on my way back home,
I passed beneath dense trees and then though,
The setting sun was at the deepest chrome,
A dark silhouette came through with me too,.
A Raven's swooped striking with its beak,
And left me wondering as to why ?
Its harsh croaks came from above the trees,
And then I heard the baby bird's cry,

That dark plumage and mysterious eyes,
Intruded into Raven's nest, crushing eggs,
Lacking vision of the higher skies,
Will the villain pay on piercing pegs?

No compassion, ready to play foul,
Raven's wraith is as bad as the owls!

79

Colours Of Rainbow

Clouds when veil the mighty sun,
Morning seems so dull and wet,
Rainy day can be much fun,
Joy that tiny drops beget;

Colourful umbs run on roads,
Footpath forgets carefree walk,
Evening croak of frogs and toads,
Resting calm of a skylark!

Scent of water freshens life,
Enjoying work isn't child's play,
Woe bygone and so is strife,
As if joys will ever stay!

Rainbow colours bring sunshine,
Vibrancy touches each mind!

80

For The Love Of Words

Deep in love with words
I keep digging through the day,
Although words fail me
Still can't help reverberate,
I am a structured poem.

81

Freedom

Sweet Maina and witty Parrot,
two pets in my mom's house;
Early morning ate chopped carrot,
and watched cat chasing the mouse.

Parrot repeated everything I spoke,
Maina would sing early morning hymn;
I would go crazy with their every stroke,
as they complimented each other in rhythm.

Getting home quick to play with the two,
always waited eagerly for the last bell to go;
Packing books fast that ended the day's blue,
saw affection in their eyes that ended my woe.

Days, months and years were gone,
sadness in their life I could slowly sense;
My thinking ability as if had sharply grown,
hiding loneliness, joys were a mere pretence.

Reflected in the songs was an unexplained grief,
craving to meet peers their own and embrace;
Freedom only could bring them absolute relief,
soft and kind they were honouring our place.

As I opened door of the cage to ease them fly,
clearly flowed deep love, for years we did share;
Reaching close, hugging to dampen my share of cry,
freedom was boon, spread wings finally afloat in air!

82

The Gift Of Life

Every day as I open my eye,
a brand new sun shines bright in the sky;
Every flower that colours my day,
keeps gloom and darkness at bay.

Every breeze that sends fragrance,
a gift of life feels His essence;
Every meal that my mom cooks,
satiates my appetite to contented looks.

Every friend waiting me arrive,
a sweet smile gives logic to survive;
Every laugh that goes in air,
an achievement shows its unique flair.

Every tear has something to teach,
as flow of emotions will preach;
Every heartbeat that speaks of love,
thrives for the peaceful dove.

Every relation has its own taste,
without these life is a big waste;
Every work is a daily worship,
wholehearted and not with a whip.

Every material thing is a lust,
never to forget mortality comes must;
Every soul that behaves kind,
sends glitter even in eyes of a blind.

Every night I pray to The Lord,
give might to the pen and let perish the sword !

83

Addictive Poetry

I suddenly wake up and it's midnight,
And my heart is still at the poetry site,
Quietly get up and look for my mail,
And then into drafts and notes I trail;

Words and sentences my passion,
Traverse my inside ever in succession,
When these get struck at synapses,
Keep giving me concurrent relapses;

Addictive poetry my first love,
As if my soul is hands in glove,
Newer rhyme with every heart beat,
Deeper in my vein flows its each streak;

Fiction or fantasy at times for a contest,
Obsessive compulsion to enter gives a stress,
For want of creative words, I get too lean,
Expressing true emotions it's serene!

84

Lonesomeness

When ghosts of seclusion haunt,
and murky clouds of gloom veil the mind;
When tears on rosy cheeks freely flaunt,
heart misses a beat and lags behind;

Must you intervene and rescue the kind,
certainly prejudiced is the sublime;
Unable to introspect as love is blind,
drowning in deep ocean of worldly mime!

85

Golden Scroll

Your golden words in divine scroll,
As the time takes its toll,
Its true copy deep in my heart,
Every moment tears my soul apart;

May I read your words aloud,
Unveil the sunshine, let go the cloud.

Still adore the first day I saw you,
Blue dress, long hair, beauty came true,
Your glittering eyes and a sweet smile,
Nothing could have been more fragile;

Slowly as I knew your heart,
You were rather better smart,
Humble to all and very kind,
I could read your intense thoughtful mind;

Even if some day far I am gone,
With you will ever stay my clone,
Forget not all our meets and treats,
Sweet and at times sour greets;

Blush on your face and rosy grace,
Icy cold winters and firing embrace,
You were looking far more bright,
Forget not our first intimate delight!

Thanks to you for keeping patience,
You have proved to be of great endurance,
Losing me shouldn't lessen your glow,
Wish time had stopped or moved slow!

Golden words today have turned amber,
Eyes wet, heart fuming to smoky chamber!

86

I Will Be Back

I actually am not the way
That now really I look,
Once a humble kind
Is now a shrewd crook,
Flower of spring once,
Now a leaf of autumn,
Fluffy flying cheerful,
Now compressed cotton;

Am I there to blame destiny?
Or the time that turned me so?

Perhaps my weak inside,
That was once my pride,
Perhaps my fading zeal,
Everyone wanted to steal,

Perhaps my lost courage,
Once my absolute rage,
Perhaps strong character,
The only strongest factor;

Do I need to ponder once again?
Or is there nothing left to gain?

Only if you send me a ray,
A hope, I won't go astray,
Only if you could assure,
My love is true and pure,
Only if you evoke a faith,
My belief was not a fake,
Only if you hold me once,
Allay fears, beat to the punch!

Do you think a fervour in life I lack?
Is there any reason I will not be back?

87

Unsung War Heroes

Glow of her youth and bridal dress,
She, at her best, was sure to impress,
He was too handsome a groom,
Any heart meeting him would bloom;

Call of duties and there he went,
Wedding day close, yet no repent,
Would be bride his greater strength,
Parents proud of their brave son;

War was on, courage was shining,
Patriotic spirit , warriors were fighting,
Weapons and bloodshed at every crease,
Brave soldiers were slaying for peace.

Hats off to all unsung war heroes,
Selfless their love for country flows,
Never ending wait for parents and bride,
Yet sacrifice for nation is a matter of pride!

88

Friends

Standing by you during all odds,
Emotive help saving from frauds,
    What are real friends for?

Sharing your big and small joys,
Exchanging gifts and all toys,
    What else are friends for?

Bearing your poetic endeavour,
Out of way doing great favour,
    What are dear friends for?

Turning your evenings bright,
Yet managing stay out of sight,
    Why do they make you crave?

With betrayed emotions you will spy,
Losing trust is not a far off cry,
Why do they break up?

With humour and wit you may win a heart,
Closer hugs enough to give a start,
What if souls are one?

The Thrill
Can grill,
The romance
Can stance,
Ethereal delight,
Losing fright,
Pure ecstasy!

89

Sweet Little Susan

Sweet little girl Susan,
Returning from school,
On her way back home,
Found a little pup alone,
Hitting car was gone,
Injured in leg groaning!

Kind hearted Susan
Brought him home
Named him Bruzo,
Took him to doctor,
Wounds healed fast,
Care best medicine!

Cattie her sweet cat,
Made friends with Bruzo,
Licked his tender face,
Cooed and soothed,
Bruzo was thrilled,
Love was a sweet pill!

Guggu, the talkative parrot,
Chirped from his cage,
Susan was a little sage,
Birds animals or mankind,
To all she was equally kind,
Her love was totally blind!

Dear child of her parents,
Her pink chubby cheeks,
A broad smile on her face,
Could reduce grief to a trace,
Her small world full of grace,
Everyone she would embrace;

One home and so much fun,
Many toys but had no gun,
Fairy appeared out of her book,
Swayed magic wand, gave her a wish,
Goodness in life never goes waste,
Never ignore anyone in a haste!

90

My Sweet Sister

HE then granted my wish,
Little sister in my lap would swish,
As if an angel stepped down the heaven,
Diamond of my eyes, sparkles to ravish,
Born today, day and month both seven!

91

Epiphany

My tender pen writes,
Takes me out of hides,
Roller coaster rides,
My emotional tides!

My life in the soup,
Humble magnificent group!

I am dreaming in fast,
Leaving behind my past,
Quick to discover,
I am on soup cover!

It's a gorgeous pun,
A real great fun!

Got warm welcome,
Scuffed out tantrum,
Anticipate friendship and love,
Warmth of hands in gloves!

Dr. Upma A. Sharma

My life in the soup,
An infectious croup!

Rendezvous face to face,
Drunk to full grace,
My cravings flourish,
To a lifetime cherish!

It's a gorgeous pun,
A real great fun!

My desires thrive,
Contrary to strife,
I am getting lost,
Well iced and frost!

My life in the soup,
A magnificent group!

My terminal Cupid,
I can't be more stupid,
An eternal abode,
I infatuate, I explode!

It's a gorgeous pun,
A real great fun!

92
Diwali - Festival Of Lights

Twinkling stars in courtyard light up the sky,
On an absolutely dark moonless Diwali night,
Sprit of festival comes in alive!

Everyone looks glamorous, in best of attire,
Colourful lights and candles glow bright,
Twinkling stars in courtyard light up the sky!

Warm Embrace puts an end to enmity and satire,
Sets off every mood exactly right,
Spirit of festival comes in alive!

Dr. Upma A. Sharma

Colour display of crackers, no fight fire with fire,
Exchanging sweets and gifts gain new height,
Twinkling stars in courtyard light up the sky!

Beauty in ideas beyond diamonds and sapphire,
Vast hearty emotions walk in equal delight,
Spirit of festival comes in alive!

Return of Lord Ram to Ayodhya we celebrate,
Worship of Goddess Luxmi, prosperity to plight,
Twinkling stars in courtyard light up the sky,
Spirit of festival comes in alive!

Dr. Upma A. Sharma

93

Muffled Cry Of An Unborn Daughter

Impregnable fortress, my mother's womb,
Beyond all evil reach, no one can intrude,
Bundled with joy, I rocked and rolled!

Little to my conscious, did I know of the plot,
To kill me inside, even before my birth,
Just because they knew that I was a girl;

Small family norm, families you design,
Male dominance, a unilateral align,
Do you think female foeticide is no crime?

Although I am no threat to a man's being,
Doused my ambitions, catered to his fragile ego,
Suppressed my desires, closed my thoughts;

I covered myself as if guilty of being a female,
Transformed myself into an art that fascinates,
Yet reave me of my right of being born?

I will now equate myself, my dear mother,
Let me once breathe in the same air;
Tears in eyes, heavy heart, a muffled cry,
I will expand your world, procreator I am!!

94

December

Down in valley, up the hills, trees shimmer in snow,
Everyone awaits eagerly for dear December,
Cherishing last year's joyous memories,
Each heart yearns to beat in fresh rhythm,
Made for each other, those cozy quilts
Beacon, as you may chill frozen till the marrow,
Envy not who received best of Santa's,
Reminisce the vibrant taps of Christmas night!!

95

My Man

Does she love me?
Does she love me not?
Does she respect me?
Does she respect me not?

When such doubts arise in your mind,
light your inside, pretence of blind,
Faith dwindles on sharp razor's edge,
confidence how can you pledge?

Mirror that constantly reflects your smile,
will testify your trust in me with pride,
Walk down the memory lane for once,
to recall taste of recent intimacy thence;

That blazing embrace how could you forget,
tender emotions, passion do you regret ?
Twilight of evenings and our dream home,
Can imagine be pyramid or memory dome?

Be sure my love for you is still young,
there is no magical moment unsung,
Recall our little one cry the whole night,
every morning awake in gleaming delight;

See my eyes brim with need of you,
blush of touch can you misconstrue?
Think what would I be without you,
Soulless, cold or red aglow?

Day we first met engraved in heart,
that gave my life an illustrious start,
Treasure your love in my every beat,
O man! You make me absolutely complete!

Do I love you?
Do I love you not?
Any doubts?

96

Life

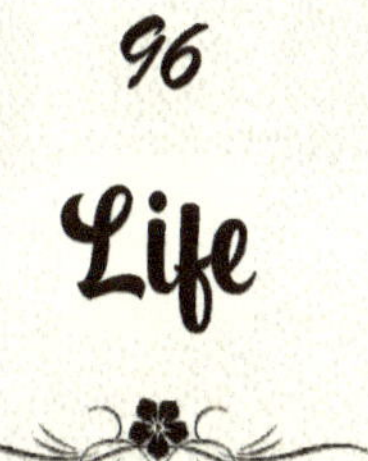

Sweet song with a vibrant essence,
Flowing flawless with a seventh sense,
Every warm, heated and iced moment,
Savour life's quintessence!

Dr. Upma A. Sharma

97

The October Sky

white and blue hyacinths
float on infinite canvas ~
water reflects by

vast as human mind
uncountable mysteries ~
paint vivid colours

immense blue gentian
camouflages to orange ~
the October sky

98

Starry Sky

As I lie on my bed
restless and sleepless,
Staring at night sky
lending twinkle to stars,
Amazed at the beauty
way they look so bright,
Those dreams of longing
vanish in insomnia;

Maybe I am in love,
maybe I was out of sight.

As I conquer my desires
yearnings reach an end,
His love in my heart
pounces to pretend,
Dreams turned to reality
sleep no more fascinates;

Maybe I am in love
and I was out of sight then.

Eyes that once sobbed dry
now the tears glitter,
On every tender blink
I fear losing these pearls,
Heart that stops awhile
and regains its flair,
Hymn that darkness sings
the starry sky enchants.

Maybe I am in love,
When dreams put to reality,
Who bothers about sleep?

99

Butterfly Sings

singing the struggle
as vibrant colours enchant ~
flutter of my wings

100

The Sweater

To a frigid wind's quiver,
Graces a warm embrace,
Of passion knitted in hot threads,
My sweater hugs his chest,
To a frigid wind's quiver.

Dr. Upma A. Sharma

101

My Final Poem

When beautiful fairies will wait
and brighter the sun will glow,
Magical essence of breeze
colourful flowers will show;
A subtle knock on
and I am ready to go.....

To meet my beloved and my dad,
who wait up in all beauty and grace,
All those I declared dead
shall bugle to let everyone know;
That I am on my way
to relive their giggles and laughter.....

Best of my friends that care
will bid holy goodbye,
My mom, my son, my sis, my bro,
for days will miss and drown in tears;
Success and achievements
throughout all laid to rest,
Every emotion and all desires
will see an end as I kiss the serene fire ....

Grieve no one as I am glad,
Liberated of all deeds and sins,
Grieve no one as I am glad,
Liberated of all fears and hurt,
Grieve no one as its nothing new,
Died and born many times,
I changed vivid costumes;

Purity of my soul
as lustrous gold,
Ready to be reborn
in a fresh avatar.

O sweet death ! Come get me!
As magical ink waits for me;
A pen and a piece of paper please,
Mind doesn't die; Words don't die;
In every new world I will write,
My final poem in this birth.......